Art of Disciplining with Love	Celestina Oniye-Thomas

Art of DISCIPLINING With Love

First published by Floating Counselling 2019

ISBN: 978-1-9161585-0-4

All scripture quotations are from the King James Version of The Bible unless mentioned otherwise and because of the dynamic nature of the internet, any web addresses or links contained in this book may have changed since publication and may no longer be valid.

The views expressed in this work are solely those of the author and **do not necessarily reflect the views of the publisher, and the publisher hereby disclaims any responsibility for them**

Tel: 07305882959

Email: Info@floatingcounselling.co.uk

Web: www.floatingcounselling.co.uk

Twitter: @Floatcounsellor
Facebook: @FloatingCounselling
Instagram: @Floating_bodymindsoul

DEDICATION

I am dedicating this book to my Heavenly Father, who blessed me with an amazing earthly father, Reverend Prince Olusegun Oniye. He had so much ambition and writing a book was one of them. My earthly father's prayer for us his children was for us to live a better life than he had and achieve more than he had, with less pain than he had endured.

My earthly father was made an orphan at the age of nine in Nigeria. He used to speak of the immense cruelty meted out by the relatives he lived with - some days he even went without food. Although as a child he knew that he was from royalty, that question, "Who am I?" remained, as it does for most humans, especially those who do not know their parents. He did not want his children to experience the physical and mental trauma he experienced, and so his parental strategy was sculpted by this. My father adopted a different approach that I have adapted to fit the world I envision for young people around me.

To it, I have added my knowledge and experience gained after over a decade of work in psychotherapeutic theories and in clinical work. This book is evidence of his unconditional love, giving spirit and kindness. I wish to pass these principles on, not only to my children, who sadly will never physically see or know him, but also to so many parents and parents to be, carers, educators and anyone who is tasked with the responsibility of caring for children. I want all to know that kindness and love is what is needed to raise a better generation.

Mo ile to ti wa ~Yoruba proverb

Know the home you are from

This I try to remind my own royalty of every day – that as princes and princesses they are beyond unique and special. As I grow and mature and watch children grow and mature, my method of parenting must change because the world around us is ever changing too. As parents we need to stop raising children for the world we were raised in. That world no longer exists, just as the world we currently live in will also cease to exist. However, what never goes out of style is resilience, empathy, emotional intelligence and unconditional love - these are characteristics we should always nurture in children. Here are some questions to consider as you read this book and think about your parenting:

Have you adopted a parenting style?
Do you know what shaped your parents' parenting style?
Why have you adopted this style?
Have you ever hit your child/ren?

Feel free to quote pages and your answers to:
info@floatingcounselling.co.uk
Instagram: @floating_bodymindsoul)
Facebook: @floatingcounselling
Art of Disciplining with Love Celestina Oniye-Thomas

INTRODUCTION

This book originally started as a chapter in another book I was writing about parenting. However, the more I wrote, the more I realised that the subject matter needed to be explored in a book of its own. I grew up in a home where corporal punishment was the norm. Like many of our generation and before, it was all I knew as a means of disciplining children. My father didn't hit us though, but used phrases like "I expected better from you," or "I am disappointed in your behaviour." In this book, when I use the word 'hit' I am referring to all forms of corporal punishment ranging from light spanking to beating.

As a Psychotherapist, I now know that hitting can cause more than physical damage. The effects of corporal punishment reach far and wide. It can create emotional distance which has a negative impact on future relationships. Furthermore, it is linked to an increase in mental health issues, alcohol abuse, domestic abuse and much more.

Corporal punishment caused me emotional issues that I had to deal with through therapy. I have had to retrain my brain to heal mentally so that I can deactivate the automatic negative thoughts, emotions and behaviours that I developed as a result. This is still an ongoing process.

This book is important for me, both personally and professionally. I disagree with hitting children because I do not like the effect it has on them. Yes, the child stops whatever they are doing the moment they are hit, but it does not correct the behaviour.

Have I ever hit my child? Yes of course – as an automatic response - especially when I am too tired to follow through on discipline. As a mother of two energetic boys, I understand why parents hit. It would be a lie to say I do not understand or that I do not want to do it. I have also yelled at them, and research has shown that shouting at young children is as bad as hitting because it triggers the same reaction of fear; I will explain the dangers of this later.

So, here, now, after my own intense personal therapy and research I cannot agree with hitting children. I have become so passionate about this topic and I believe more people need to understand the effects of hitting children that I decided to turn that chapter I was writing into this book.

This book will discuss and offer realistic alternatives to physical discipline. I hope these will allow us as parents to raise healthy and resilient children that know love and can show love in a healthy way to self and others. Any parent who reads this book should be aware that their actions can cause trauma generations to come. So many things lay dormant in our DNA and actions like hitting can turn dormant traits in our DNA, alive. This book will not immediately put an end to hitting, but let it compel you to find alternative means of disciplining your children.

CONTENTS

CONTENTS

SECTION ONE

Senegal

'Haste and hurry can only bear children with many regrets along the way.'

~Senegalese proverb

Firstly, I would like to say that as humans, we are not perfect.

Perfection is unattainable. However, as parents if we keep trying our best then we might catch excellence. - Celestina Oniye-Thomas

I want each parent to catch their excellence and allow their child to do the same for themselves. When parents hit their child, it's usually out of annoyance and never love. I know this might make some shake their heads and say "No, I do it out of love".

TASK

Next time if you hit your child, afterwards, assess yourself and try and remember your thoughts before you hit the child. Did you think "I love you my dear" or was it more a case of "This child is testing my patience," "I must show you who is boss," "This child is irritating me," or "This child is embarrassing me?"

Write a personal journal of your thoughts below.

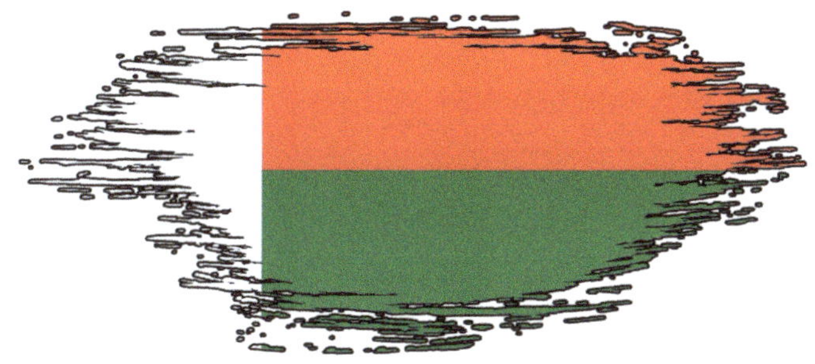

Madagascar

'Words are like eggs.

When they hatch, they have wings.'

~ Madagascan proverb

No rational human strikes another, especially a child, in a calm, loving state. Doing so indicates an anger problem. In many ways, it teaches a child that this is the best way to express emotions like anger and annoyance and solve disagreements. We tell children not to fight but to use words, yet we hit them. Children learn by what they see, and not just by what you say.

To justify hitting as an act of love, the parent often highlights the child's bad behaviour:

"You never listen."
"I will teach you to listen today."
"I am doing this to teach you, to help you, etc."

The parent is communicating their annoyance and coating it with love and help, but this is translated by the child as, "I'm bad" or "I do not deserve love right now." The above does not need a Psychotherapist to decode how negative this scenario is. It sends mixed signals:

- Love is painful
- Help is painful
- The people who love me will always cause me pain
- To love others, I should cause them pain

This creates psychological wiring in the child. As they grow up, life events may teach them that these statements are true or, alternatively, contradict these statements. Whichever way, there is an impact on relationships with others, because the contradiction causes an internal confusion. They regress and become a child living in an adult body. As humans, we resist confusion by wanting to prove to ourselves that our inner self is right. This can cause the regressed adult to go around hurting others to prove that she or he is right.

Hurt people hurt others.

Behaviours like these are subconscious, so in some ways it is pointless to ask why some adults continue to dish out hurtful behaviour. This is not to make excuses for them, but rather alert us as parents to know that our actions will certainly mould our children's brains and adult behaviours. We create damage that they then have to undo to stop the cycle of pain. Once we know this as parents, why would any of us want to create that situation for a child we love?

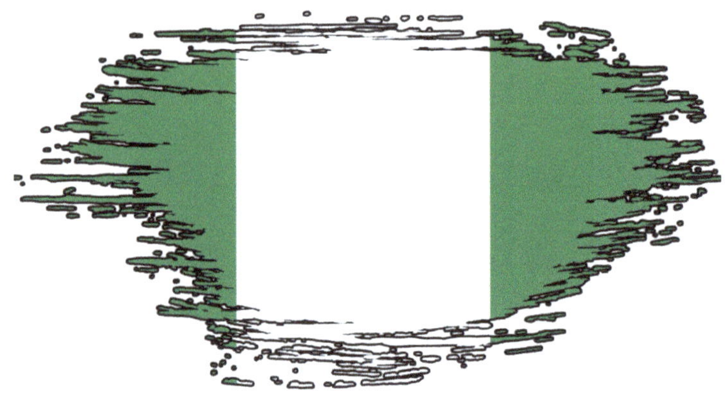

Nigeria

'When there is no enemy within, the enemy outside cannot get in.'

~Nigerian (Yoruba) proverb

Parents almost always feel bad after hitting their children and this has an impact on their self-esteem. In my work with parents, I have learnt that we all want to feel more confident in our parenting ability and be free of guilt especially after disciplining our children. Children pick up on this and can use it to their advantage, which defeats the purpose.

If a child knows you hate to discipline them, or you feel bad about it, they will use this to get out of dealing with the consequences of their behaviour. Jeremy Todd, Chief Executive of the charity Family Lives said, “We would never endorse smacking as we feel that there are much better ways to communicate with a child. Parents who contact us say that smacking comes as a reaction; it is not a controlled moment. They often speak of their regrets; it is not something that gives a good feeling.”

If your method of discipline does not feel good to you and your child, then what is its purpose? What are you teaching each other? Discipline won’t always feel good, but should it hurt or demoralise?

As a parent, are you doing your true best? Is your type of discipline appropriate for your child? If the answer to both questions is yes, then there should be little guilt.

Example**:** Your toddler wants to play with fire, which of course is dangerous, so you move them. The child cries. No parent wants their child to cry. However, of course it's more harmful for them to play with fire, so there's nothing to feel guilty about.

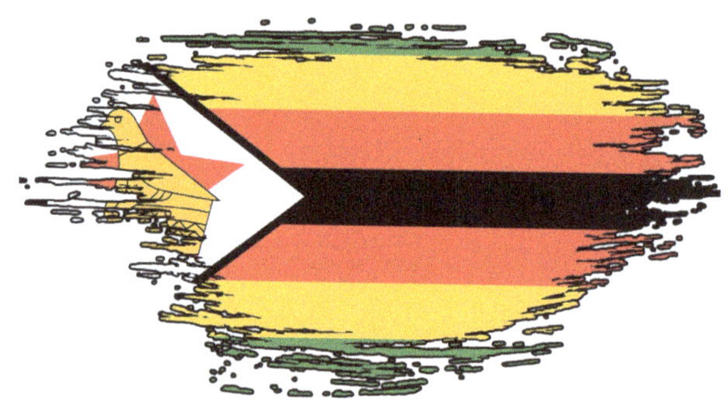

Zimbabwe

'The axe forgets but the tree remembers.'

~Zimbabwean ~(Shona) proverb

Why might parents repeatedly resort to corporal punishment even when it results in guilt and achieves nothing? There are several reasons and here are, in my opinion, the three main ones:

First, many parents simply do not know how else to discipline their children - this is the only way they know. Therefore, this book is important because it presents alternative, realistic methods that work.

Secondly, and this is the most common rationale I hear given in support of corporal punishment - many feels that it did them no harm. When I observe the individuals who support this viewpoint, they usually demonstrate difficulty in communicating their own emotions, needs and desires. They may display inappropriate responses as we often do when we allow our subconsciousness to surface. If I were to slap them, their reaction, understandably, would be anger or fear. However, how would they manage this emotion? Would they be able to think it through before responding? If we teach our children to feel an emotion, then assess and evaluate it carefully before reacting, we will then be raising children who grow into emotionally intelligent adults.

Emotional intelligence is a concept that was popularised by Dan Goleman in 1996. It's the ability to know one's own emotions, to recognise those of others, to discern what is required for a particular situation and environment, as well as the personal benefits of doing so.

It's the ability to label emotions correctly and appropriately and put that knowledge to use when navigating one's thoughts (cognition) and behaviour.

Let's stop for a minute or two and think of what makes a parent hit their child. It's usually when we cannot find the words for our emotions, so instead we immediately react and hit. I know this explains just how I've felt when I've hit my child. However, when children do this, we call them naughty and…hit them. To be clear, I have hit one of my children, the eldest, three times in his life, none was a rational moment, and no justification.

Finally, the internal voice of the parent is that of the child who has learnt that 'hurt people hurt others, love can be painful,' etc. It's this voice that drives their behaviour as parents. In my counselling room, the hardest thing to shift in my client's cognition are these voices. The negativity that was spoken and acted out into their lives by their parents sticks to them and becomes their own voice to themselves and others. Our brain does not forget the good, the bad or the ugly. Everything is stored, we then react to them when triggered subconsciously.

SECTION TWO

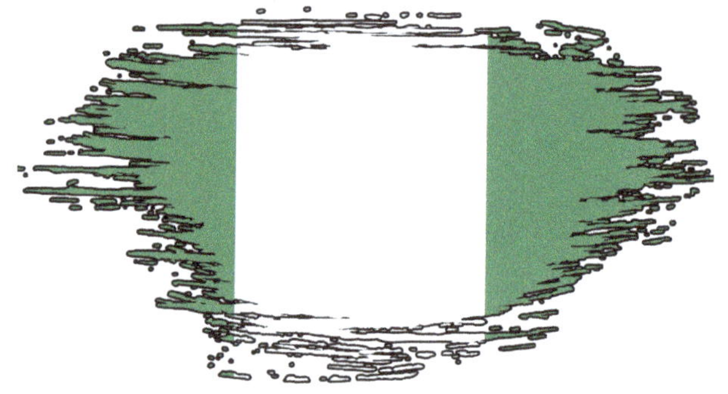

Nigeria

'A child who fears beating will not admit that he played with the missing knife.'
~Nigerian proverb

It's so important for parents to find more loving ways to discipline their children, and this starts with communication. Simply put - talking! Our children need to know right from wrong and they must be taught to own up to what is wrong to make things right. We should not put them in a position to lie to us, hurt themselves or others or feel ashamed. We must talk to them from a place of love so that they can talk to us especially when they have done wrong.

When we hit a child without any explanation, the child is left confused, not knowing why what they did was wrong, why they should not do it again, and what the right thing to do was. Many parents would say "the child knows", but this is an assumption. I have been with my husband for almost 15 years, and I still have to talk to him about most things. He's not a mind reader, so why should a child be one?

Write your answers to the questions below:

How long is/was your longest relationship?

____

____

____

____

____

____

Do you or did you still talk about some things?

____

____

____

____

____

____

Write a list of things you still need/ed to talk about with your current or last spouse/partner that you thought they should know.

____

____

____

____

____

____

Communicate, communicate and communicate some more. This is necessary in any relationship be it husband and wife, employer and employee or parent and child. Assumptions and instilling fear do not work. Effective communication works. Showing love and compassion helps.

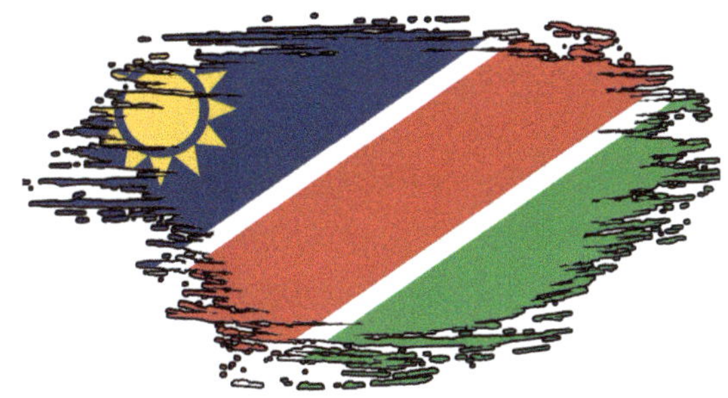

Namibia

'Let the first urge pass, the second will come.'

~ Namibian proverb

Hitting teaches a child to hit and models how conflict is dealt with. The parent-child relationship should be built on a healthy foundation. This is a theory proposed by Eric Berne in the 1960s. In one way or the other, we all internalise our parents' or main caregiver's behaviour. So, if the parent-child relationship when growing up is healthy, the child will internalise that. What do I mean by this?

Let me break it down

We all have an adult, a child and a parent inside of us. If your parents responded to your tantrums and behaviour with corporal punishment or verbal abuse, then it is likely that as an adult you will associate parenting with pain. You may internalise verbal abuse as parental and may even verbally abuse yourself to communicate with yourself - 'Why am I so stupid?' 'I can't even make a relationship work,' 'I can't do anything right,' 'I'm so stupid,'. With a healthy parental relationship as a foundation, the conversation with self would go something like this, 'I'm not having a great day so maybe I should take it easy today,' or 'It's a shame that relationship didn't work out. Guess it's a lesson learnt.'

The inner voice is supportive, loving and motivating just like the parents' voice was.

Ethiopia

'The fool speaks, the wise listens.'

~Ethiopian proverb

The power that parents and primary caregivers have over their child/ren is significant and far-reaching. If this relationship is unhealthy, and there are other positive parental role models in the children's lives, they may still grow into resilient and well-balanced adults that can overcome the damage from the primary parental model.

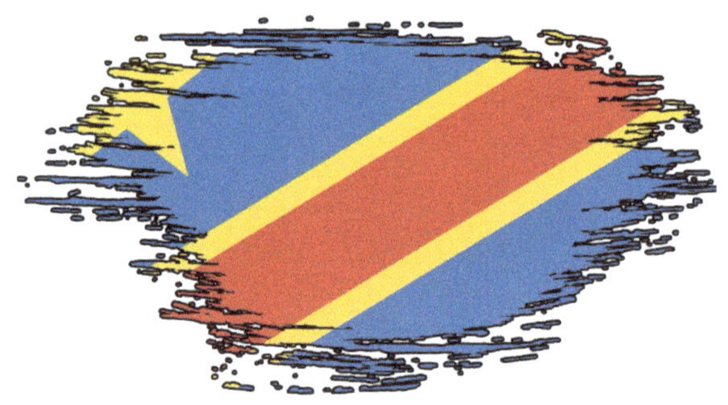

DRC Congo

'The art of negotiation is acquired from childhood.'

~ Congolese proverb

When children grow up, they may be more forgiving and understand that the parent did not know any other way (this can also be seen as Stockholm Syndrome, I will explain this more soon), or they may keep that resentment. They may see through the pain and either see that the parent meant it as love, or as hate.

Why would any parent want to raise a child that grows into an adult that is unforgiving, especially to them?

Often parents label a child who is bold as rude, when, the child is learning to be an assertive and thoughtful adult, the type of adult that we want our children to be.

The only way to raise a child to become an assertive adult is by allowing that child to communicate with you through talking and asking questions. At the same time, they need boundaries and healthy ones at that, they need to learn to be tactful, allowing them to be children. Most important of all, they learn from watching us deal with conflict and communicate with family members and strangers.

Example: My son (eldest) would nearly often narrate back to me, word for word, things I had said to him in the past. At a young age, everything is important. My son will even negotiate discipline too – "Can I eat pancakes then go wash the plates?"

We as parents may find this frustrating and it can be. However, if we don't allow our children to learn to articulate themselves, then when and how will they do so?

The child who is restricted in their use of the normal communication channels will eventually turn to people who will allow them to be heard. Alternatively, they may grow to become aggressive or come under the negative influence of those that do harm. We parents must acquire better ways to communicate with and parent our children so that no one else will do this for us.

Zambia

'The first may not necessarily arrive first.'

~ Zambian proverb

Some parents feel that because they **think** they came to no emotional harm as a result of corporal punishment, it's also appropriate for their children. However, we all know how different we as adults are, and children are no exception. Just because something works for one doesn't mean it will work for another. It's important to know your child and know them well to understand their psyche and select the optimal method of discipline that yields real results without harming them emotionally and physically.

The other thing to be mindful of is that a lot of people did indeed suffer emotional damage because of corporal punishment but do not recognise that they did. That negative internal voice I spoke of earlier can lead to a negative outlook on life and love and this often stems from childhood issues with the primary caregiver such as angry discipline.

I know of men and women who physically abuse their husbands, wife's or partners and admit to having anger problems. However, they will argue that even though they were beaten as children (or witnessed an abusive relationship between their parents), that has had no influence on their current behaviour. Such men or women were not taught to resolve conflict and so they continue to deal with conflict in the only way they know how. They emulate their parents treating their spouse like the child they once were.

Of course, other factors come into play, but there is no doubt that abusive relationships in adulthood stem from the same in childhood.

This is not to blame abusive people's behaviour on corporal punishment they received as a child. However, that way of a parent showing love and discipline is unhealthy and can transpire in an adult to adult relationship, where one adult in the relationship treats the other one like a child, thereby removing their adult control and self-autonomy as a parent would to a young child. I also know people who accept different types of abuse, including physical and sexual abuse from their partner as a way of life because of their internal voice to self which says, "love is painful and s/he loves me and does what they do (abuse) because they love me".

Stockholm Syndrome is also another reason. It's a name given to a condition which causes hostages to develop a psychological alliance with their captors. The name came from an incident in 1973, when four hostages were taken during a bank robbery in Stockholm, Sweden for six days. The outcome was alarming as the people taken defended the people who took them as hostages and even later spoke of love and later married each other. Stockholm Syndrome is now a term used when an abused defends their abuser. This perfectly explains individuals who defend their partner, their parents or others who have abused them.

This syndrome has seen those abused give excuses for abusers, it has seen those abused stop police arresting abusers, and it has also seen people who have been abused join abusers to abuse others. In the same vein, many people who were hit, defend this as a valid form of discipline and then go on to hit too.

SECTION THREE

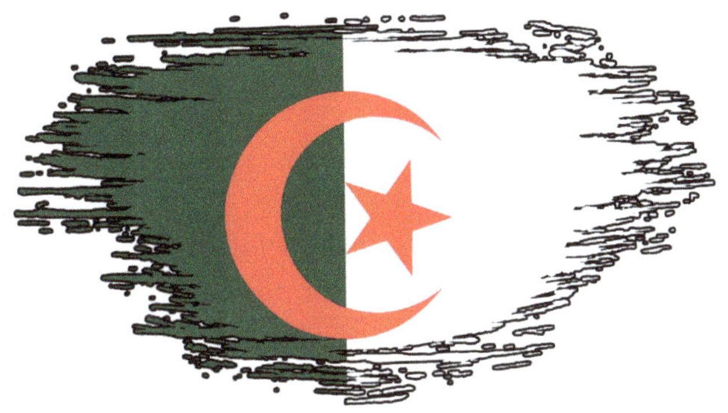

Algeria

'Speak kindly or refrain from talking.'

~ Algerian proverb

"I don't really hit or beat my child. I only spank them, and I don't spank hard."

I understand why at times a little spank on the hands feels like the best option – it's quick and easy and stops the unwanted behaviour, usually immediately. However, even this seemingly innocent response of a little soft slap especially on the hands has its dangers. Children use their hands to explore their environment. Hitting this essential part of the body teaches the child that their hands can encounter danger, discouraging them from exploring and therefore developing as they should. It also remaps the brain to think that exploration is painful and wrong, so they should avoid it as much as possible.

This was demonstrated through some psychological research with 14-month-old toddlers. One group of toddlers was spanked lightly on the hands for touching forbidden objects, and another group of toddlers (control group) had the objects simply taken away from them. A few months later, the children who were spanked were less skilled and less adventurous in their environment than the control group. Imagine what opportunities the children who were spanked could miss out on - feeling new textures, trying new foods, missing out on professions in the arts or music or engineering or the soothing effects of just touching. It's difficult to imagine how something so seemingly innocuous as a soft slap on the hand can have such an impact. How many other things do we do that can reshape a child's brain to that extent?

The results of this study really highlight how mindful we must be as parents about the effects of corporal punishment and indeed any of our words and actions.

Zambia

'Today's bush is tomorrow's forest.'

~ Zambian proverb

As parents, we usually hit our children usually to stop some unwanted behaviour. Whilst that behaviour may stop temporarily, it's not a guarantee that it will improve.

What hitting does is cause pain which the brain remembers and tries to avoid. As there is usually no communication between parent and child about why the behaviour was inappropriate, the child only remembers the pain. They will then do what it takes to avoid the pain which may include lying about the behaviour. In this situation, we can see that an even bigger problem has arisen – dishonesty – on top of the initial behaviour. If corporal punishment continues in the absence of communication, the problem simply becomes bigger and bigger, laying a foundation for all the issues that we have discussed in previous chapters.

What else could children do to avoid the pain of corporal punishment? ***What did you do when growing up to avoid corporal punishment?***

Send your answers here and quote this page:

info@floatingcounselling.co.uk

Instagram: @floating_bodymindsoul

Facebook: @floatingcounselling

Our children represent this planet's future. No matter what that future holds, integrity, morals and ethics will remain necessary and we should ensure that they retain those characteristics by raising them with compassion and love.

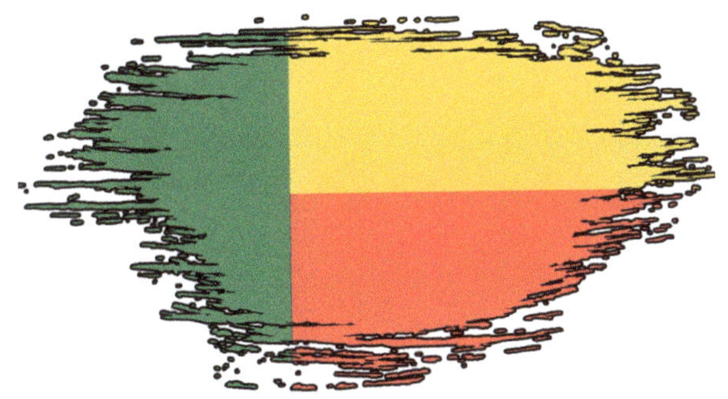

Benin

'The world is a journey, the after world is home.'

~Beninese proverb

Research has shown that children and adults learn from what they see and hear and, most importantly, through practice. Therefore, practical work is important in school and university, and why employers place such importance on experience.

How can a medical student become a practicing doctor without…practical experience? So, we must be mindful of what we show our children, the way we speak with them and the way we behave towards them.

Humans internalise (as discussed earlier) what is said to them and practice what they see.

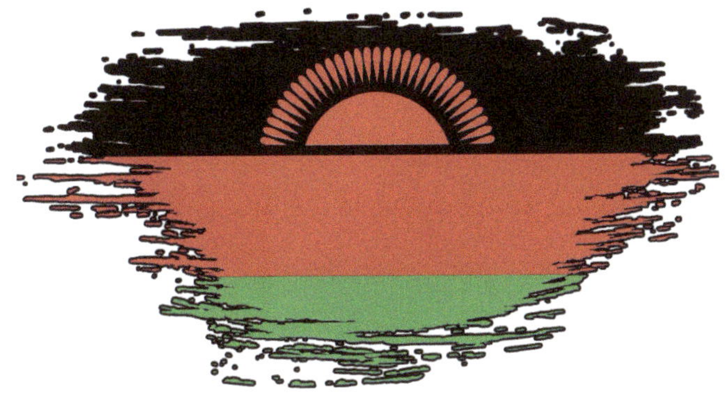

Malawi

'What is coming does not beat drums.'

~ Malawian proverb

As we've seen, hitting a child can limit growth through inhibiting exploration not just physically, but also mentally. The other effect is it simply makes the child feel bad about themselves which in turn feeds more bad behaviour. If the parent or caregiver has no insight into this and they continue with corporal punishment, the child feels increasingly worse, and the result is a never-ending negative cycle.

Egypt

'Repetition teaches even a donkey.'

~ Egyptian proverb

Numerous pieces of research have proven time out works better than hitting children. Research has also shown that hitting children does not facilitate good behaviour. One of these studies was from Dr Paul Frick from the University of New Orleans who carried out a study on 98 children and their parents with his team. The results showed corporal punishment had no positive outcome on both the children and their parents. Time out for younger children led to better behaviour and more positive outcomes.

Taking electronics or toys from older children, as well as extra chores for older children worked better than hitting or threatening to hit.

Equatorial Guinea

'A good wind is no use to a sailor who doesn't know his direction.'

~ Equatorial Guinean proverb

There is a thin line between outright abuse and hitting a child. In the United Kingdom, (as of when this book was published) it is not against the law to hit a child so long as it is not with an object and does not involve kicking and punching. There should be no imprints or scars too, which of course depends on skin complexion. It is more difficult to see imprints on a darker complexion. So how can the parent or carer or anyone else measure if their corporal punishment is abusive or not? If there are no imprints, does that mean no abuse has taken place? Does crying mean the line has been crossed to abuse? If there is no kicking or punching, but hand-hitting only, is it categorically not abuse? If you hit the face (the head) or bottom only is that acceptable? We know that hitting the head of especially young children can damage the skull, but no imprint made, but damaged caused?

What's your opinion? Is hitting abuse?

____

____

____

____

____

____

____

What country are you in and what is the law on hitting children?

____

____

____

____

Send your answers here and quote this page:
info@floatingcounselling.co.uk

Instagram (@floating_bodymindsoul)

Facebook (@floatingcounselling)

In law, there is what is called the 'thin skull rule'. It basically explains that everyone is different, and what does not harm one person can harm another.

Example: Someone who has a bad heart is frightened suddenly and dies as a result, while another scared in the same way is unharmed, laughs it off, and life goes on. Some people have illnesses they do not even know about. Hitting someone can bring on an illness that lay dormant in the body. Someone with thin blood can be badly bruised with a little spank and could even die from being struck. Some communities allow other people to discipline (punish) their children physically, without knowing if that child has an illness that can be triggered.

It is important for us as parents to find alternatives to disciplining our and other people's children. Corporal punishment is not the answer.

SECTION FOUR

Kenya

'The past years are in the moonlight, the years to come are in darkness.'

~ Kenyan proverb

Hitting induces fear and children should not fear their parents. Therefore, it is so important *not* to do it.

Fear induces the Fight, Freeze, Fawn or Flight response which is activated by stress hormones such as cortisol and adrenaline. These get the heart pumping blood faster around the body and glucose released to, for example, the muscles which are needed to run. The adrenaline makes the body more alert and glucose gives energy. All this is in preparation to…fight or fly. It is the survival instinct that originates from the age when humans hunted for dangerous animals; this instinct was needed to escape if they were in danger – it was needed to survive. Alternatively, fear can lead to freezing, where someone is so gripped, they are unable to respond because the brain starts to shut down, or the brain sends a message to the body that to freeze is safest to survive Fawn also known as people pleasing, abused people do this and learn it as a way to survive, to be on their best behaviour to minimise abuse.

So, we can see how creating a situation where our children fear us can have the opposite effect to what we desire as parents. Our children should not want to run from us, nor should they do things just to please us, instead they should be their authentic self. They can also end up reacting inappropriately in other situations. For example, if at school they are disciplined or if in a situation that creates a feeling of fear, they may resort to fighting, instead of having a conversation about how they feel. Releasing the hormones meant for survival can also damage the brain, the body is not created to be expecting or triggered into survival on a regular basis. When you use corporal punishment as a form of discipline for your child, you trigger the brain to get used to releasing the hormones. So when there is no danger the body might still releasing it.

When you are watching television and something dangerous happens, even though the danger is not real, your brain reacts to it as if it is real. In fact, therefore movies and television shows have age ratings to ensure young people are not exposed to violent scenes that can impact their brain and body negatively. Your heart starts beating fast and stress hormones are released.

In real situations, sudden acute of sustained violent situations can lead to a type of brain damage called Post Traumatic Stress Disorder (PTSD). When the brain recalls dangers everywhere inappropriately, the body gets ready for battle with the release of hormones and the fight or flight syndrome. Feeling jumpy and scared is something that those with PTSD and children who experience corporal punishment have in common. Later in life, they may grow to see life in general as a fearful situation. The one way to counteract this is to always discipline with love and never use physical punishment.

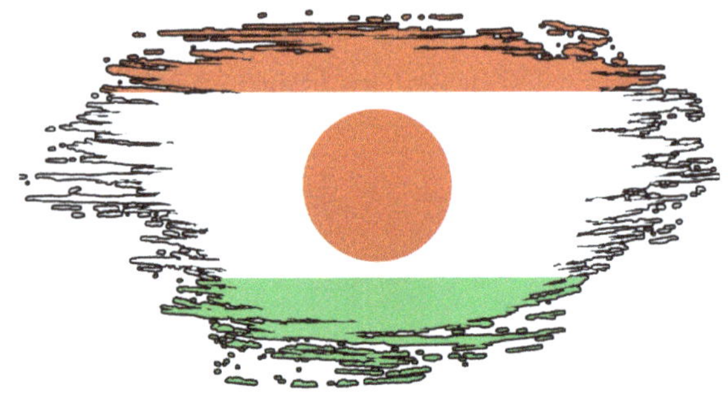

Niger

'You cannot shave a man's head in his absence.'

~ Niger proverb

Here is more on the physiological effects of hitting. When a child stops their behaviour after being hit, it's not because they realised it was wrong but because the brain froze. Other senses are then affected. For example they may not hear the instructions you give, nor may they be able to speak. This is fear.

When the brain shuts down into survival mode, the hippocampus is affected. The hippocampus is the part of the brain that stores memories. It also controls emotions and the autonomic nervous system which are bodily functions that do not take conscious effort to control, such as breathing. In a fearful situation, the hippocampus goes into overdrive resulting in, for example, faster or incontinence breathing (holding your breath unknowingly). The situation that creates fear is imprinted in the memory bank.

If you hit your child or witness a child being hit after reading this book, watch the child's response and act so as not to repeat it. Ask yourself:

What was your child's response?

What was your response as a child when you were hit?

Research suggests that the brain of a child that has been repeatedly hit is damaged, with less grey matter in the brain. Lack of grey matter has been linked to numerous mental disorders and illnesses like bipolar and schizophrenia, as well as alzheimer and dementia. It can even lead to a lower IQ and emotional intelligence. To find out more about these studies follow Dr Stacey Patton on www.sparethekids.com

Ethiopia

'When the heart overflows, it comes out through the mouth.'

~ Ethiopian proverb

Many parents who favour corporal punishment may claim that using strategies like sitting in the naughty (I do not believe any child is naughty, so I refrain from using this word to describe a child, or their behaviour) or silent corner and timeouts do not work.

What is important to understand is that any healthy method, if understood and applied appropriately and consistently can work. Every door has a way of opening - some you have to pull; others push and yet others slide. If you try to push a door that needs to be pulled, it won't open, yet it works just fine. In the same way timeout administered in the right way for a child can also work perfectly!

SECTION FIVE

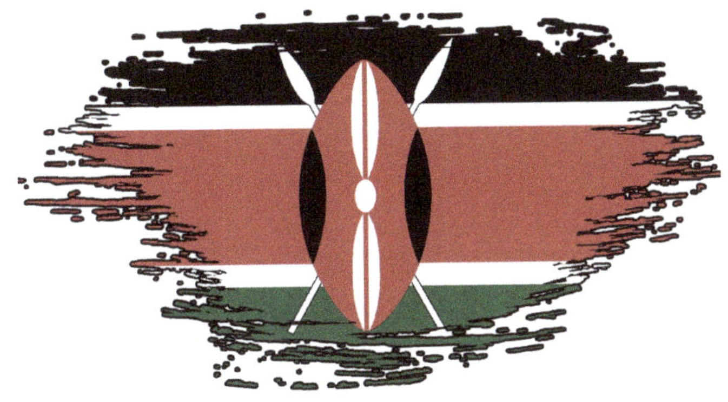

Kenya

'When you take a knife from a child, give him a piece of wood instead.'

~ Kenyan proverb

Some parents claim that explaining to a child why a certain behaviour is wrong would be futile because they just would not understand. Instead, for them, hitting sends a clear message. The question is on what basis is the presumption made that communication won't work and corporal punishment would? This boils down to the fact that hitting produces an immediate response – the behaviour stops. Talking to the child requires the adult to exhibit self-control to initially control their anger. If that adult was raised by parents who used corporal punishment, they were mostly not taught to use communication to resolve conflict and so know nothing else. The fact is, it does not take too much time to teach a child to understand what appropriate and inappropriate behaviour is, but it is time well-spent.

Any human being, regardless of age or background, can communicate and respond to communication from another. It's about understanding how to speak to that person. I have worked with special needs children from toddlers to 18-year olds (some who could not talk or even communicate in any way, not even sign language) and we all understood each other, when I learnt to communicate on their level.

Parents need to learn how to communicate with their children in a way that children understand, not the other way around. Step into your child's beautiful world.

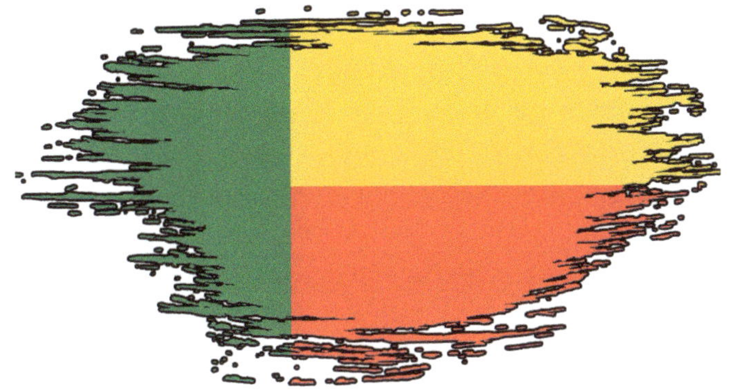

Benin

'Fear a silent man.'

~ Beninese proverbs

As parents, our main objective is to raise a child that can grow to think for themselves and process information appropriately; a child that is emotionally nourished, confident and lives by a sound moral code.

As discussed earlier, children disciplined by corporal punishment generally only learn what to do to not be hurt or caught. If they are not caught in the act they can continue with that behaviour because they were not always taught about why their behaviour was wrong, the potential consequences and alternative ways to respond.

This is where strategies like using a timeout can work as they give both the child and the parent a chance to sit and think about their behaviour and actions. After stepping out of the timeout, the parent who has also had a chance to calm down, speaks to the child to reinforce an understanding of why their behaviour was wrong. As this conversation is taking place, the child's hippocampus (where memory is stored) records it and with consistency in this approach, this strategy becomes the accepted norm.

Hitting does not give space for conversation and reflection, and hippocampus is not activated in a positive way.

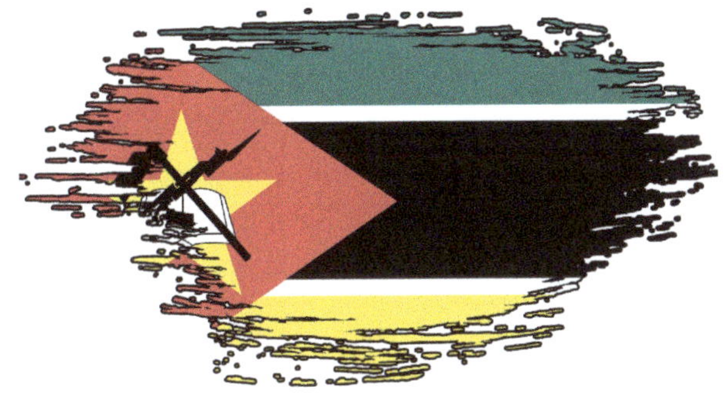

Mozambique

'There is no shortcut to the top of a palm tree.'

~ Mozambican proverb

Bullying and abuse entails inflicting harm on or intimidating someone we perceive to be more vulnerable than we are, e.g., someone smaller, etc. However, when parents do the same to their children, it's called discipline.

Is it okay to mistreat those that are younger, smaller and weaker than we are? The answer is no, yet in using corporal punishment, we are doing just that and the contradiction it presents for children is potentially damaging.

Were you ever bullied? How did it feel?

Jamaica

'If you don't hear, you must feel.'

~ Jamaican proverb

Society reinforces that for boys, being violent is what makes a man. 'It is not lady-like to raise your voice,' but men can do it?

Hitting reinforces violence and teaches that this is the right response to disagreements. When a father hits his daughters, he is teaching them that men will cause her pain. When a father hits a son or his wife, he is teaching his son to hit his own family. When a mother hits her children, she is teaching her children to do the same.

Hitting your child reinforces violence and teaches them that hitting or inflicting pain on others who disagree with you are appropriate.

How many men do you think died due to suicide this year alone?

____

____

____

Compare that to the number of women who complete suicide and then compare it to last year's figures.

____

____

____

What do you think leads men to suicide?

____

____

____

Were they trying to punish themselves or their family and friends?

____

____

____

Men find it harder to voice their emotions, as the society is less tolerant of them showing their emotions than it is with women doing the same. It's therefore important that parents allow their children, especially boys to cry. We need to let them know that there is nothing wrong with emotions and tears. This goes a long way to their growth into balanced adults. It also teaches them to communicate effectively and be empathetic to others.

There is a high percentage of suicide among men. Three out of five suicides are men, and this is partly linked to an inability to communicate their needs. Therefore, creating an environment where communication is a component of the disciplinary strategy is so important. It can prevent future disasters, it can prevent the death of your child.

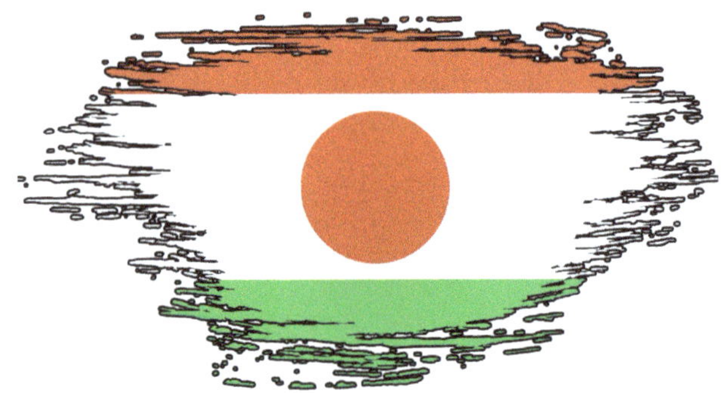

Niger

'He who does not mend his clothes will soon have none.'

~ Niger proverb

Parents cannot predict how their actions will affect their child. The occasional hitting on a background of a loving relationship may be what a child remembers. The child raised on corporal punishment as a child may go on to reject that with his own family. Another may perpetuate and justify it later.

As parents we must remain aware that we are raising future generations, not just the next one. Our child will be someone's husband, wife, mother or father. How we raise them will have a significant impact on their relationships with the rest of the world and how they will raise their own children, if they have one.

SECTION SIX

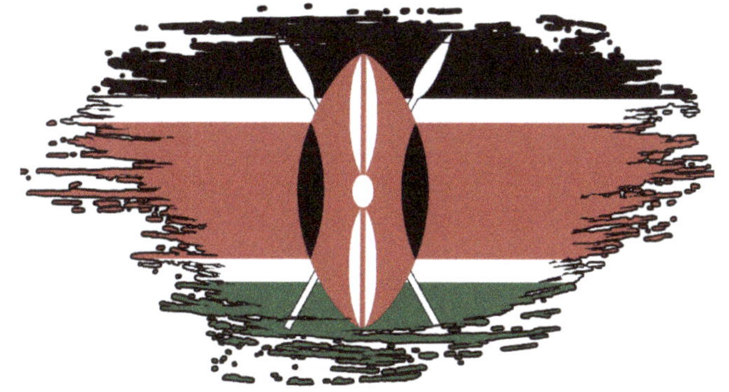

Kenya

'We have not inherited this land from our ancestors, instead we have borrowed it from our children.'

~ Kenyan proverb

Pain rewrites DNA. **Yes**, you read that right. Research has shown that our DNA can respond to life events and the environment including pain, our mental state (and nutrition) and the changes are then passed on to our children. This may explain why what may appear devastating for one is a walk in the park for another. Everyone has a different stress bucket. What does this mean for corporal punishment?

Exactly as we touched on in the previous chapter. If the brain is constantly in survival mode, this too can lead to changes in DNA. Emotional pain can have the same effect. Research also shows that colonialism, genocide, slavery, the holocaust and other such experiences can induce a PTSD that rewrites DNA. Our genes are as alive as we are and represent an imprint of our life experiences. It's therefore important that those whose ancestors may have been exposed to events that could have caused PTSD should avoid using corporal punishment to reduce the risk of further damage to the DNA of future generations.

To find out more about this research, check out the work of Professor Judy Atkinson and her book *Trauma Trails* and the work at the Institute of HeartMath in Boulder Creek, California. She has carried out two decades of research on epigenetic changes and transgenerational trauma.

One point that she highlights is that love and appreciation can help individuals heal and grow from the trauma, with their DNA imprinted with memories of how to cope in difficult situations.

My work with my clients also helps them understand the power of their DNA (also known as DNA activation), to deactivate the negative and activate positivity and healing, the beginning of it can be through mirror work, also known as soul work.

This conclusion supports that what a child needs to grow and learn is not pain but love and appreciation for who they are and the good they do. Disciplining a child with love and respect will allow positivity to be imprinted in their core and this is what they pass on to their children in their DNA and hippocampus.

Zambia

'A child not exposed to the world thinks that his/her mother is the best cook in the world.'

~ Zambian proverb

Parents often use punishment as a form of discipline. However, these are two very different processes. How are they different? Let's look at the definitions:

dis-ci-pline -noun - training that makes people more willing to obey or more able to control themselves.

pun-ish-ment -noun - the infliction or imposition of a penalty as retribution for an offense.

You can see the difference in the meanings, right? Below is a table that lists some of the features of each act.

Punishment	Discipline
- *Physically and emotionally painful*	- *Meant to guide and help a child learn to self-regulate*
- *Imposes power, strength and control*	- *Builds resilience*
- *lowers self-esteem, worth*	- *Builds self-esteem*
- *Embarrasses, discourages*	- *Teaches respect*
- *Frustrates the person being hit and person hitting*	- *Heals*
	- *Emotionally healthy*
	- *Emotionally supports and facilitates trust*

YOUR TURN!

What do you think are the main differences between the two?

Punishment	Discipline
-	
-	
-	
-	
-	
-	
-	
-	
-	

Ask other parents you know what they think?

Tell them about this book because they need it too

Parents discipline primarily based on their fears for their child's future. Read the statements below and take time to answer the questions either mentally, or better yet, by writing them down.

Your child steals. What are your thoughts?

Do you worry that the behaviour will continue, they turn to a life of crime and end up in prison?

Your child talks back to you. Do you worry that your child will have no respect for authority?

Explore your fears. Talk through them the next time you talk parenting with your spouse, partner or a friend. Alternatively write them down below.

Send your answers here and quote this page:
info@floatingcounselling.co.uk
Instagram:@floating_bodymindsoul
Facebook: @floatingcounselling

Are your fears about:
1) what your child has done in the here and now
2) you, or,
3) what others think of you and your parenting skills

____
____
____
____

In answering the above questions, I hope that we as parents realise that we should discipline not based on our emotion of fear, but based on the need to positively shape the behaviour of our child.

SECTION SEVEN

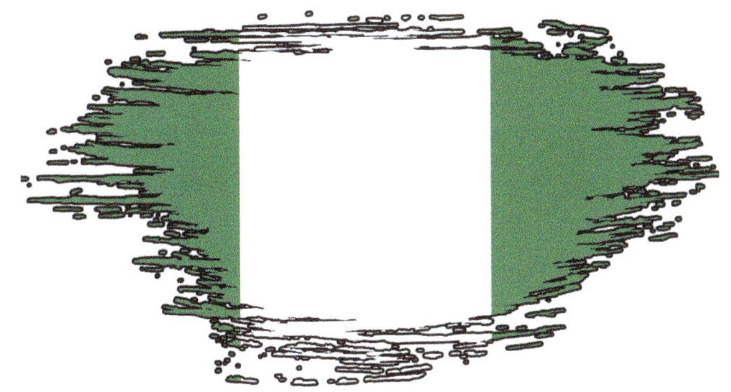

Nigeria

Madness that is inside a child, beating will remove it.'

~ Nigerian proverb

The Bible and Corporal Punishment

As a born-again Christian and a child of a late Reverend, I grew up around Christians who quoted scripture to justify the use of corporal punishment. As my own father did not follow this line of thought, I had no experience of him doing the same.

However, as I grew up and started to explore The Bible independently, I couldn't find consistent evidence to support corporal punishment. I even studied Greek and Hebrew, the original languages the bible was written in. Below are three scriptures that were often quoted as I grew up:

Proverbs 13:24 - *He that spareth his rod hateth his son: but he that loveth he chasteneth him betimes (diligently)*

Proverbs 29:15 - *The rod and reproof give wisdom: but a child left to himself bringeth his mother to shame*

Proverb 22:15 - *Foolishness is bound in the heart of a child, but the rod of correction shall drive it far from him.*

These scriptures are now embedded into a well-known proverb by Nigerians (Yoruba tribes) which I used to open this chapter.

Let me break these scriptures down because contrary to what some Christians believe, these scriptures do not give permission to beat children.

During the periods covered in The Bible, shepherds used rods and staffs to:

1) Count sheep
2) Shepherd them, especially up hills
3) Inspect them
4) Lead them to food, water or safety
5) Chase wolfs and wild animals away from sheeps

Occasionally, angry and tired shepherds may have struck a sheep, but this was not the purpose of the rod. Striking them would induce fear which will cause them to run off. (Luke 15: 4-5) says that a shepherd who had 100 sheep and if one was lost, the shepherd would not rest till that one is found.

So clearly, rods and staff were used in the care and guidance of sheep, not to hit or hurt. These were actually instruments of protection and care. When it comes to children, The Bible refers to discipline and not punishment. There is just one verse that refers to punishment:
Proverbs 23:13-14 - *Do not withhold discipline from your children. If you strike him with a rod, you may well save his soul from death.*

Hebrews 12:6-7 refers to both discipline and punishment but not to physical punishment: *...the Lord disciplines those he loves, and he punishes everyone he accepts as a son. Endure hardship as discipline; God is treating you as sons. For what son is not disciplined by his father?*

Hardship does not mean physically hurting a child or anyone for that matter. In fact, The Bible speaks of raising children with love, kindness, encouragement and calmness. The fact that some Christians misinterpret the Word, I think that says a lot more about these parents than the Bible or God. Here is more biblical evidence against corporal punishment.

Colossians 3:21 - *Fathers do not provoke your children, lest they become discouraged.*

Ephesians 6:4 - *Fathers do not provoke your children to anger but bring them up in the discipline and instruction of the Lord.*

Proverbs 19:18 - Discipline your son, for there is hope; do not set your heart on putting him to death.

There are so many other parts of The Bible that talks to parents and adults about how to be with their children. It's all about love. Discipline yes, but not in anger and not to provoke or hurt the child. Christianity is love and humility (meekness) and nothing else.

Rwanda

'Only God generates. Man, only educates.'

~ Rwandan proverb

There are however many scriptures that make it clear that hurting our bodies hurts God:

1 Corinthians 6:19-20 - *Do you not know that your bodies are temples of the Holy Spirit, who is in you, whom you have received from God? You are not your own; you were bought at a price. Therefore, honour God with your bodies.*

1 Corinthians 3:16-17 - *Don't you know that you yourselves are God's temple and that God's Spirit dwells in your midst? If anyone destroys God's temple; God will destroy that person; for God's temple is sacred, and you together are that temple.*

So, in summary, God does not advocate inflicting pain on a child's physical or mental body, but instead asks that we discipline our children in love. As far as I can see, God's words forbids us to hurt anyone's body, including that of our children.

SECTION EIGHT

Zambia

'Consistency enables one to achieve his/her goals.'

~ Zambian proverb

To achieve results in anything, consistency is important. Discipline is no different. It also requires a committed and consistent approach for results to be seen.

With this final chapter, I want parents to see that discipline can be achieved quickly without inflicting physical or emotional pain. There are several age-appropriate strategies that can be used. I have selected five that have been researched and shown to be effective in positively changing behaviour for the long-term.

The Naughty Corner

As naughty has negative connotations, I refer to this as the 'time-out corner' or just 'time-out'. How does this work?

Give your child a countdown to stop their behaviour. Count slowly in a firm low voice telling them that if they don't do so by count five (or three), they then start a time out. You don't say anything more - just send them to time out.

If they step out of time out before you say they can, send them back without a word and repeat this until it stops. Some may cry and scream in time out and that's fine - stick to your plan.

It's helpful to use a timer that they can see too. Children have no sense of time so if they can see that it will end soon, they settle down. From May 2021 you can order an effective timer from my website www.floatingcounselling.co.uk As you use this method more, you will see them start to process and understand that they can avoid time out if they change their behaviour.

Ensure there are no toys or other forms of entertainment in the vicinity. This defeats the purpose of having thinking time.

Time out for the child is also time out for you. You can take a moment to calm down. You can also enjoy a drink undisturbed, use the toilet alone, eat chocolate without having to share...the list of things you can do in this impromptu me time is endless!

You will be surprised by how much children hate time out because it takes time. My child immediately jumps as soon as I say I'm going to start counting. The counting now usually doesn't even get to start because they stop undesired behaviour! Very rarely do I make it to five.

Here are some other rules:

- Stick to your word
- Count firmly
- Don't count too fast or too slow - be fair
- At the end of time out, remind them why it was necessary

- Ask them not to repeat it

Hug them to show them that you still love and care for them, because after discipline young people often feel as if they are hated. Reassure them that you didn't like their behaviour (name the behaviour or act) but you still love them. If the behaviour is particularly bad, no countdown is needed. Immediately send them for time out but follow the same rules at the end.

Teach Natural Consequences

If your child spills water on the floor, they mop it up. Easy right? No! More often than not, the parent will rush to mop the water up. Children clearing and cleaning often creates more of a mess and it takes far too long. We figure we are going to have to clean up after them anyway so we may as well do it the first-time round! However, if your child missed out on the natural consequences of an action, like mopping after themselves, it would remove the chance to change the behaviour that led to the situation in the first place.

Follow through on this with every behaviour that you need to modify in your child.

Yes! Ignore!

There are some things that can be ignored as not everything needs a reaction. Remember to work out the behaviours your child may do for your attention. What can you ignore? Generally, behaviour that is not serious or dangerous.

Example: You ask your child to do something and they say no. Ignore the no and ask again or try another way to get the child to obey. Being offended, shouting at the child, and using time out won't work. Time out in particular will only confirm to the child that you use it for meaningless things. It then fails to be effective when you need it to. It's therefore just the no that gets your attention and your child will recognise it and use it.

Remember:

If you notice your child displays a certain behaviour for attention, be prepared for it and prevent it, by offering positive quality time together. If child uses no to respond to your requests, then rephrase your question so that they can't use no as an answer!

You: Put your coat on please.

Your child: No.

Then, try this:

You: What do you want to put on first? Your coat or shoes? The child only has two options! None of those options is no.

If your child is seeking attention, he/she needs something and that cannot be ignored. There are many reasons for this but at the core is that they want your care, undivided attention or love. So, why would you punish them for that and what should you do?

Firstly some children draw more to quality time as their love language, in fact all children need quality time as this is usually how children see love.

The only solution is to give the attention so that it does not become overwhelming to you the parent. It also allows your child to connect with you. If your child does not feel connected to you, they won't listen or respect you as they grow older and become more independent. If you do not pay attention to the needs of your child, they will seek attention elsewhere. Children need to know that they are loved and are important to us. However, there is no denying that we live in a world of busy now, busy tomorrow, busy every day, and so below are quick ways to get your needs and those of your child met healthily and lovingly through...play.

Playing together

This is a fantastic way to give them that attention and here's how you can do it:

- Set a timer for ten minutes (or whatever you feel appropriate but make it at least five minutes). I have a set of timers for you on my website, 1 minute, 3 minute, 5 minute, 10 minutes, 15 minutes and 30 minutes

- You can choose to join in their play or watch. The key thing is to focus on them with no mobile phone or laptop or iPad involved.

- Get to their level - so if they are sitting on the floor, you sit on the floor. If they are sitting in the chair, sit next to or opposite them, giving them enough space to be, but close enough to have an intimate moment.

- You can even create this intimate moment at meal times and even if you are not eating you can sit with them.

- Make sure you are looking at them warmly and showing that you are enjoying the time spent together.

- If you have other children, make it clear to them that it's currently X's turn and their turn will come. Every child needs this undivided attention.

Alternatively, ask someone to be with the other children while you spend time with one. This will help during discipline too because the child is more likely to obey and listen to you, and this does not mean they would not test the boundaries. Every human does that, but with consistency in your attention and love it only gets better.

PACE - playfulness, acceptance, curiosity and empathy

This final strategy puts everything together and can create a secure bond between child and parent without compromising discipline. It remains effective even when the parent is not physically present.

We must remember that children right up to the teen years are learning to regulate their emotions, some even after teen due to a variety of reasons. Every child

initially finds it hard to do this and express their emotions appropriately. Without a secure relationship with a parent or carer, they may cover up emotions, misunderstand them or express them in an unexpected manner. Children on the autistic spectrum find emotions even harder to understand and regulate, so be mindful of this and be patient.

For example, most adults who are in tune with their emotions will know that anxiety may manifest as a stomach-ache. With the same emotion, a child will simply say “my stomach hurts,” because they have not yet matured emotionally to be able to connect the two. The gut is usually where anxiety and fear are expressed because it’s one of the places the body automatically shuts down during survival mode as discussed earlier.

The same hormones are released for both excitement and fear. Feeling these emotions can sometimes turn to anxiety because of confusion and lack of secure attachment to the main caregiver. Therefore, it is important to communicate with children to explore what they feel and why they feel what they do. They may then be able to separate and understand their emotions.

Example:

You: Go to bed.

Your child: My stomach hurts.

Your child may be anxious about the dark or sleeping in a new room or going to school the following day.

Explore this, be patient and find out if there is an underlying problem that can be fixed.

This whole book has been screaming solutions. Parenting simply needs love, empathy, an accepting nature and promoting and enhancing positive behaviour instead of zooming in on negative traits.

Playfulness is using a light tone to speak to your child instead of irritation. Playing with your child is good but being playful in your responses when they misbehave doesn't mean you are encouraging bad behaviour, nor is it sarcasm.

It just means you soften your responses but still have the objective of changing an unwanted behaviour. As we know, hate fuels hate; so, if your child is having a tantrum, shouting won't help. Instead, just be calm in their storm.

Remember they are learning how to be from you.

Acceptance is allowing the child to know that they are accepted no matter what. This again does not mean refusing to discipline and accepting negative behaviour from the child; this lets the child know you receive them and not the behaviour and that you love them and not the behaviour. This needs to be communicated verbally and in the right tone, as well as cemented with your demonstration of love (e.g., that hug) once discipline is over.

Some parents will discipline but spend the rest of the day and weeks later still talking about the child's negative behaviour. Discipline the child and let go. This way of parenting allows the child to know you love them unconditionally. They will also take this way of being into their relationships. For any successful relationship to last, forgiveness is a must. If children are not allowed to forgive and do not feel forgiven, forgiving others would be harder as they grow older.

Curiosity is having a non-judgemental mind, tone and method of questioning that does not come from a place of annoyance or anger. If questioning comes from a place of sadness or anger, do not expect an answer.

The point is to get the child to understand why they did what they did and why it was wrong. Learning can only be done in a safe zone. Children may sometimes know right from wrong (do not make assumptions as discussed earlier) However, they will not always know why they may have done what they did. This is why timeout is good because it gives them some sort of thinking time.

Allow the child to process the whys and help them regulate their behaviour from their core. The older they get and the more this is done, the more they can communicate why they took a certain course of action.

They must also not worry about being judged. If they do, they may feel shame and children lie when they feel shame, or when they know they will be disciplined.

This can be avoided with PACE, and it is better they process the reason and communicate honestly than grow up without integrity lying their way through life.

Empathy is staying with the child's emotions and letting the child know it is not too much for the parent. The parent remains sad if the child is sad, but in a manageable way. Allow the child to come to terms with their own emotions and accept it. It is okay to be sad, but do not mask it or ignore it. This allows the child to know and feel they are not too much.

***Example*:** You ask your child to eat but instead they scream and throw it all over the floor. Instead of reacting in anger, you can say any of the following:

- Wow, are we playing food fight?

- What made you do that?
- Food gives you energy. Now you will be tired.
- I am sad that you have done this.
- What are we going to do now?
- You have to clean it up.

Then get the child something to clean the floor. If they are still young, clean with them but not *for* them.

There is no shouting, no hitting and the child does not get an opportunity to behave worse.

They also see you calmly deal with the situation. You also teach them that you do not hate them, but that the behaviour is not acceptable. You can then put the child in timeout after cleaning. However, the cleaning is also part of disciplining as it teaches that there are natural consequences for their action.

Sounds simple enough right? Good!

I have left spaces for you to write and observe your own behaviour

Go do it and let me know how it goes by writing to me at:

info@floatingcounselling.co.uk

IMPORTANT!

All these strategies will work if you follow these four rules:
be consistent, keep calm, show respect, make sure you follow through

Nigeria

'If you tell a child off with your right hand, you pull the same child towards you in love with the left hand.'

~ Nigerian proverb -Yoruba tribe

To find out about healthier, more loving and caring ways to discipline your child, I am offering you a free 25-minute consultation.

Join the Impact Parenting Tribe on Facebook and Send an email to me info@floatingcounselling.co.uk with the barcode at the back of this book and some basic information about you, your child and the concerns you have.

Please be honest about your fears. It will all be confidential, I will then send you a link through which you can book the free consultation directly with me.

For more offers visit: www.floatingcounselling.co.uk

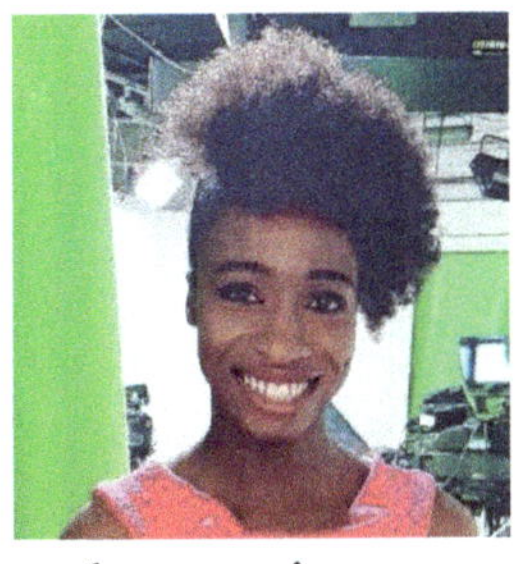

About the Author

Celestina Oniye-Thomas is a multi award winning qualified, insured and practising psychotherapist, coach and motivational speaker. Using her professional expertise and experience, one of her main objectives is to empower parents to consciously raise the next generation, by dealing with their own past traumas

She is the founder of the international organisation Floating Counselling which provides counselling, mentoring, coaching and food parcel services to vulnerable people. Celestina has been a clinical practitioner in the United Kingdom for over a decade and has worked in schools as a supply teacher including at special needs school and those for children with behavioural challenges. This reflects her passion to equip young people with the tools that allow them to be the best that they can be. Celestina also carries out humanitarian work, and that along with this book shows her commitment to giving those in need the opportunity to live their best lives. Her guiding principle is that without opportunity or a sense of belonging, it's difficult to achieve goals.

'The child that is not embraced by the village will burn it down to feel its warmth.'

~African Proverb

To find out more about Celestina's charitable support, speaking engagements and projects in the UK and Africa please visit:

www.floatingcounselling.co.uk
Instagram: @Floating_bodymindsoul
Facebook: @Floatingcounselling
Twitter: @Floatcounsellor
LinkedIn: Celestina Oniye-Thomas

www.ingramcontent.com/pod-product-compliance
Ingram Content Group UK Ltd.
Pitfield, Milton Keynes, MK11 3LW, UK
UKHW062313290726
14090UKWH00018B/1045